THE SPARKLING JEWEL OF NATURISM

T0347789

Selima Hill grew up in a family of painters in farms in England and Wales, and has lived in Dorset for the past 30 years. She won first prize in the Arvon/*Observer* International Poetry Competition with part of *The Accumulation of Small Acts of Kindness* (1989), one of several extended sequences in *Gloria: Selected Poems* (Bloodaxe Books, 2008). *Gloria* includes work from *Saying Hello at the Station* (1984), *My Darling Camel* (1988), *A Little Book of Meat* (1993), *Aeroplanes of the World* (1994), *Violet* (1997), *Bunny* (2001), *Portrait of My Lover as a Horse* (2002), *Lou-Lou* (2004) and *Red Roses* (2006). Her latest collections from Bloodaxe are *The Hat* (2008), *Fruitcake* (2009), *People Who Like Meatballs* (2012), shortlisted for both the Forward Poetry Prize and the Costa Poetry Award, and *The Sparkling Jewel of Naturism* (2014).

Violet was a Poetry Book Society Choice and was shortlisted for all three of the UK's major poetry prizes, the Forward Prize, T.S. Eliot Prize and Whitbread Poetry Award. *Bunny* won the Whitbread Poetry Award, was a Poetry Book Society Choice and was shortlisted for the T.S. Eliot Prize. *Lou-Lou* and *The Hat* were Poetry Book Society Recommendations. She was given a Cholmondeley Award in 1986 and a University of East Anglia Writing Fellowship in 1991, and was a Royal Literary Fund Fellow at the University of Exeter in 2003-06. Her pamphlet *Advice on Wearing Animal Prints* (Flarestack Poets, 2009) won the Michael Marks Award.

As a tutor, Selima Hill has worked in prisons, hospitals and monasteries as well as for the Arvon Foundation and London's South Bank Centre. She has worked on several collaborations with artists including: *Parched Swallows* with choreographer Emily Claid; *Point of Entry* with sculptor Bill Woodrow; and *Trembling Hearts in the Bodies of Rocks* with performance artist Ilona Medved-Lost.

SELIMA HILL

The Sparkling Jewel
of Naturism

BLOODAXE BOOKS

ISBN: 978 1 78037 103 0

First published 2014 by
Bloodaxe Books Ltd,
Highgreen,
Tarset,
Northumberland NE48 1RP.

www.bloodaxebooks.com
For further information about Bloodaxe titles
please visit our website or write to
the above address for a catalogue.

Supported by
**ARTS COUNCIL
ENGLAND**

Cover design: Neil Astley & Pamela Robertson-Pearce.

Printed in Great Britain by Bell & Bain Limited, Glasgow, Scotland, on
acid-free paper sourced from mills with FSC chain of custody certification.

To Sparky

ACKNOWLEDGEMENTS

Acknowledgements are due to the editors of the following publications in which some of these poems first appeared: *Moth, Poetry London, Poetry Review* and *The Times Literary Supplement*; and to the 1930s Health and Efficiency movement for the title.

The cat on the cover is for Ciara.

CONTENTS

Doormat

15 Me

16 China Doll

16 I Do It

17 Silk

17 The Lake

18 Lapdog

18 Dachshund

19 Saw

19 Skating

20 Punishment

20 Bath

21 Perfection

21 The Way You Walk

22 In the Orchard

22 Sunshine

23 Goose

23 Bedtime

24 The Migration of the Antelope

24 Courage

25 Aviation

25 Roses

26 Pornographic Novels

26 Dog

27 Shrimp

27 Hair

28 Sunday Afternoon in the Flat

29 Why I'm Here

29 Flowers

30 PARADISE
30 Salt
31 The Gift
31 I Certainly Won't Mention the Dog
32 Hygiene

Happiness Is Just a Waste of Time

35 The Little Girl
36 White Rabbits
37 The Girls They Like
37 Crocodiles
38 Fly of My Youth
38 Hazelnuts
39 My Sister's Dachshund
39 Shampoo
40 Yesterday
40 Little Car Parks
41 Spiders
41 Kitten
42 Midday
42 Shopping
43 The Man Who Stands Outside in the Dark
43 Guinea-pigs
44 Toffees
45 Trout
46 Never Go to Sleep in a Lake
47 Polystyrene
47 The Sick
48 Girls
48 Our Naughty Kittens
49 Articulated Lorries
49 Soft Cliffs
50 Dumb

50   The Man with Scented Hands

51   Hope

51   Young Women

52   Georgia O'Keeffe at Lake George

53   The Seven-Stone Champion Chicken-Wing Eater

54   Bears

54   Owlets

55   Trains

55   Tomorrow

56   The Dream

57   The Music Teacher's Nephew

57   Entomology

58   Boyfriends

58   Very Tall Herons

59   Eucalypti

59   Whelk

60   Glittering Flies

60   Heifers

61   Odonata

61   Ponies

62   Naturism

62   Torquay

63   Facts and Figures

63   The Lives of Our Fathers

64   Everything

64   Rats

65   What We Want

65   Dustmites

66   Paranoia

66   Iris

67   Evening Out

67   What It Feels Like to Feel Like Me

68   Paradise

Blowfly

71   Bridesmaids
72   Bath-time
72   Meringues
73   Wives in Hats
73   Teddybears
74   Ducks
74   Tennis
75   Hubcaps
75   Nail-varnish
76   Salvation
76   Jam
77   Married Women Even at Their Gloomiest
77   Breakfast Time
78   Profiteroles
78   God
79   Snails
79   Bungalows
80   Representatives from the Milk Marketing Board
80   Hopes
81   New Clothes
81   Horses with Gold Teeth
82   Tobogganist
82   Potatoes
83   How to Fish
83   Desert Orchid
84   Tomorrow
84   Whiskers
85   Married Women on Holiday
85   Travelodge
86   Sunbathing

86 The Nights of Married Women

87 Sorrow

87 Songbirds

88 Snowflake

88 To Pedal Round an Ornamental Lake

89 The Less They Know

89 High Dependency

90 With Their Bony Fingers

90 Married Women in Their Long Coats

91 Funeral

DOORMAT

Me

To me, I'm me. To you, I'm someone fabulous,
someone you're so jealous of it hurts.

It hurts not only you but also me.
It hurts so much it's best to ignore it.

China Doll

Like a china doll with real hair
staring straight ahead as if it's seen

something that it shouldn't have seen,
you are very beautiful. I'm not.

I Do It

I don't know what it is
but I do it.

I do it all the time
without thinking.

I do it in your face.
I can't help it.

Silk

Everybody thinks you're really sweet.
They love the way he dresses you in silk.

You stare at him with your staring eyes.
You and he are repellent to me.

The Lake

Every time he hurts you again,
it makes you think you want to be like me

swimming upside down in the lake
with nothing to disturb me but lily-pads.

Lapdog

He never seems to grasp the simple fact
that you're a human being. On the contrary,

anyone would think you were a dinner-set
or little lapdog bred to sit on laps.

Dachshund

Unlike me with my funny nose
and funny yellow ringlets, you've got nothing –

nothing but an elongated dachshund
no one likes. *Enjoy it while you can.*

Saw

If you speak, people back off –
like they would if a saw spoke.

Skating

We circle round and round the freezing rink
and some of us improve and some don't

and some, like you, who dare to ask the question
nobody dares answer, don't try.

Punishment

Punishment, punishment, punishment.
Nothing in your life will come close

to what it feels like to feel punishment.
Here it comes. It's sweeter than they think.

Bath

Having spent the afternoon asleep,
it stretches its short legs and goes upstairs

and hops into the bath to catch the drops,
or would do if it could, but it can't.

Perfection

All you've got
to make him even notice you

and make your life worth living
is perfection.

The Way You Walk

You walk as if your shoes are full of stones,
as if you know nothing is worth having
and everyone has given up waiting
and everything you long for holds you back
and no one thinks you're wanted and you're not
and all you want to do is not stand up
and everywhere you go you go to sleep,
still strapped inside your startling snow-white underwear.

In the Orchard

Like a tortoise
searching for a husband,

you search the orchard
for the perfect plum.

Sunshine

Every time it shines, it shines on me,
it shines on me and on my wedding-dress

which doubles in your nightmare as a helipad
that's constantly swarming with helicopters.

Goose

You want to love me but you don't know how.
You follow me around like a goose.

Finally you abandon hope
which you should have done years ago.

Bedtime

Every evening
when you go to bed

it jumps into your arms
because it knows

what it feels like
to feel lonely.

The Migration of the Antelope

To envy the migration of the antelope
but not to move,

to think you are a doll,
is simpler than to risk being human.

Courage

It's not because I bully you. I don't.
What I do is simply ignore you.
I do it all day long. In the end

you haven't got the courage to protest,
never mind the courage to begin,
not even to begin, to forgive me.

Aviation

Like a man in love with the sky
who spends his days waiting for an aeroplane,

you wait for God, and, while you wait, you nervously
dab your various spots and cuts with Germolene.

Roses

You say that roses taught you how to pray.
You also say, in tears, that every day

you forget His love. You also say
you know He makes you cry *for a reason*.

Pornographic Novels

When is it OK to kill small insects,
to go downstairs,
to hammer on the door,
to plan to club your rumba-loving neighbours
and all their rumba-loving friends to death
and when is it OK to line your living-room
with pornographic novels?
No one knows.

Dog

It looks as if a golden-brown magnolia-bud
has been transformed into a little dog –

people even think it's a *real* dog!
Its velvet tail smells and tastes of shrimp.

Shrimp

I probably won't mention the shrimp
and I certainly won't mention the dog

swimming through the duckweed like the fingertips
slipped inside your hair as if to say

they'd never been so happy in their lives.
I'll talk about your toiletries instead.

Hair

When I think of you I think *hair*
and how your hair is like the shiny hair

of china dolls whose hair is real hair
and what a doll with silver hair would look like

and then I think how long you have been waiting
for me to even notice that they're there.

Sunday Afternoon in the Flat

To find you dressed from head to toe in moths
that may be very beautiful to look at
but have no language to address me with

and even those that flutter on your face,
instead of things to say, have only maxillae,
to find you dressed in moths as in a veil

would tell me more about what's going on
than finding you're prepared to sit and talk to me
but only about nothing else but beauty products.

Why I'm Here

I'm here to make you weep and I do.
I make you weep again and again.

(*Weep* not *cry* – you're not a child, you know!)
You weep as if to say *it's all over*.

Flowers

You walk and talk and eat
very slowly

as if you had no energy for anything
except the observation of your flowers.

PARADISE

The little dog trots into the bathroom
that we can smell from here smells of PARADISE

and jumps into the bath and licks the drops
as if the taps were nipples but they're not.

Salt

You must have many reasons to be frightened.
Of me, I mean. I wonder what they are.

Sometimes I can't bear not to ask you
but I never will. *Wound. Salt.*

The Gift

When you feel miserable you tell yourself
this is what God *wants* you to feel

which makes you feel even more miserable –
miserable, devoted and confused.

I Certainly Won't Mention the Dog

I certainly won't mention the dog
and I certainly won't mention the lake

and I certainly won't ask if I can help you
because I can and I don't want to.

Hygiene

You fold your clothes
and make them into piles
and wonder why it has to be so difficult.

Your armpits
are like stainless steel armpits.
Nothing really matters except hygiene.

HAPPINESS IS JUST A WASTE OF TIME

The Little Girl

The little girl may be little now
but very soon her rabbit will be dead

and she will have become a grown woman
baking cakes again and again.

White Rabbits

If a friendly man with two white socks
peeping from his shoes like two white rabbits,

who keeps a set of marbles in his ears
and chocolate ballerinas in his pockets,

whose house is home to various small poodles
some in urns, some in cardboard boxes,

if such a man drives a little girl
round and round his garden in a pedal car,

let's hope that little girl is not me;
or, if she is, let's hope I'm not a poodle.

The Girls They Like

The only girls they like are the sleepy ones
that might as well be blue they're so white –

the blue of someone sitting in the snow
who can't remember how to get back up again.

Crocodiles

They're even cooler than the crocodiles
that lurk in nurseries in the roots of mangrove swamps

crunching dentures, watches, hats and body parts
and that's why God has given them lingerie.

Fly of My Youth

It spends its day at work on rump and tail,
bows to no one, will not be my pet,

is interested in nothing else but *cows*
and even when it lands on my lip

I know I can't compete with a cowpat
or walk about with jam up my nostrils.

Hazelnuts

Naked children with their mouths like moths
that come at night and sip the tears of elephants

confined to stalls and thrown a few oranges
stay awake and swallow sleeping-pills

the size and shape of nodes the size of hazelnuts
glinting in the sun like sunlit caplets.

My Sister's Dachshunds

The neighbour's dachshunds
live on minced chicken breasts

like children who can only draw
octopi.

Shampoo

The little girl sitting in her bath
underneath a turban of shampoo

would rather be a duck because a duck
never feels naked when it's naked.

Yesterday

When tomorrow comes, it skips away
and turns itself discreetly into yesterday,

a day in which a pair of tiny hands
still searches for the nail-varnish bottle.

Little Car Parks

Little girls should wait – like little car parks
that don't know what it is they should be waiting for;

that nobody expects to do anything
except befriend a butterfly or two.

Spiders

The music teacher touches my hand
while outside in the corridor the cleaner,

leaning back against a warm pipe,
is picking spiders off her yellow duster.

Kitten

Squeezed into a curious fur dress
that squeezes him so tightly he wakes up

and sees it's not a dress but a dream
in which he can't remember how to sleep,

the music teacher blinks like a kitten
that no one ever wants to let go.

Midday

At twelve o'clock the tarmac-scented sunlight
is in the park burning the babies

and blinding and encasing the mothers
whose cries ring out like very high-pitched bells.

Shopping

A little girl
learning how to shop

is like a poodle
learning how to sunbathe.

The Man Who Stands Outside in the Dark

The man who stands outside in the dark
with toffees in his hand can go to Hell

where helicopters clatter back and forth
making sure no one's got their clothes on.

Guinea-pigs

At mealtimes
we kick our skinny legs

like guinea-pigs
racing tiny tricycles.

Toffees

Toffees, reels, catgut, feather flies,
collecting words with silent g's like *gnat*,

fish-hook stoppers, monkfish whose decay
lend them an air of sanctity, the sanctus bell

but mainly toffees
should attract me to him.

Trout

He drove me through the night like live trout
until the night he lost the will to live,

refused to eat, refused to even look at me
and something there's no word for yet kicked in

and all he wanted was to take my hand
and find a quiet place to be alone with me

and feel what it's like to be the man
he never thought he'd let himself believe in.

Never Go to Sleep in a Lake

Never go to sleep in a lake
and never be alone with a newt

and never feed a parrot sliced tomato
if what the parrot wants is sliced *banana*

and never wander off into the desert
where even snails struggle to survive

and never ever sleep on the mattresses
besotted kings incapable of sanity

tell you you'd be stupid
to pass by.

Polystyrene

If little girls
were made of polystyrene

they'd be less pink
but even squeakier.

The Sick

Some of them
eat what they are given

while others
simply throw it at the cook.

Girls

We eat and grow and multiply
like flies

but unlike flies
we know we are replaceable.

Our Naughty Kittens

To carefully unhook
our naughty kittens

is not as hard
as to unhook our bras.

Articulated Lorries

Only little girls become women.
Articulated lorries, hymenoptera,

even polyester turns to dust
but only girls first become women.

Soft Cliffs

Soft cliffs loved by small invertebrates
are not a soft as adolescent girls

who mournfully acquire the shapes and sizes
of cows in halters trying not to calve.

Dumb

We've got to be dumb,
we've got to forget everything

and when we have forgotten
it will come.

The Man with Scented Hands

No one sees the man with scented hands
place the bucket back inside the van

and no one sees or smells the missing girl,
her velvet dress glittering with fish-scales.

Hope

If what we mean by hope is, first, hope
and then the pleasure of foregoing hope,

of waking up to find our hearts are broken
like broken snail-shells, then I hope.

Young Women

Girls have got to stop being girls
and learn to be young women and to constantly

monitor everyone around them
and give them what it is they really want.

Georgia O'Keeffe at Lake George

I've no idea if Georgia O'Keeffe
went swimming there herself or even wanted to

or why Lake George or why the name *Lake George*
makes me want to swim there but it does –

to swim until the f's and e's dissolve
and nothing else makes sense except geese

who paddle round the lake in twos and threes
and never have to read or spell anything.

The Seven-stone Champion Chicken-wing Eater

What about forgiveness? Is forgiveness
morally adequate as a response or isn't it?

and why does the scrawny seven-stone champion chicken eater
insist on eating her way through all those chicken-wings

and what do Croatian and raincoats have in common
and is the verb *to copulate* correct

and are things basically good and basically workable
or are they not and is it true or isn't it

that she ate one hundred and eighty in twenty-one minutes
and, be that as it may, when she vomits

I know we know exactly
what she means.

Bears

Girls who are too fat
should keep their heads

sealed up in bags
like new bears.

Owlets

Adolescents are like big owlets
queuing up for their first flying lessons

who never want to hear the word 'owlet'
(or 'adolescent' in their case) again.

Trains

We watch the days go by like the man
who sits beside the track watching trains:

we sit and watch like him, but not for trains,
we watch for something small, that we might miss.

Happiness

Adolescents
are like chosen pigs
angels carry into dark woods

and as we journey on we understand
Happiness
lies ahead like piglets.

The Dream

When you're young you neither know nor care
that being young is nothing but the dream

of someone who's too young to be old enough
to be the woman she's too young to be.

The Music Teacher's Nephew

Sleeping with the music teacher's nephew
is like sleeping with a very small flannel –

a flannel that's too small and grey to know
this is, or was, the future we've been waiting for.

Entomology

Being me is all very well
but still it's not the same as being loved

and, even if it is, being loved
is not the same as being loved *enough*,

as being loved so much you feel love
not only for yourself but for others,

even for myopic entomologists
obsessively pulverising laurel leaves.

Boyfriends

They crawl across our skin like promised snails
but all we want to do is do our hair

that shimmers with bright trails like the trails
of inconsolable gastropods everywhere.

Very Tall Herons

Even though they look as if they hate us,
even though they actually do hate us,

even though we're minding our own business
when down they come like very tall herons

pretending they're too elegant to fish,
we'll have to learn to love them in the end.

Eucalypti

The eucalypti rattling in the wind
are boring all the hedges of the neighbourhood

by telling them where and how they're peeling
and what it is they hate about themselves.

Whelk

Baby whelk grow up to be whelk,
hippopotami hippopotami,

little girls grow up to be women
and bricks and boys grow up to be brick walls.

Glittering Flies

They glitter in the sun like tiny men
searching in the sand for tiny women
to lure into their tiny hotels

where every day they eat themselves so sick
being sick's an end in itself;
they glitter most of all on those who sunbathe.

Heifers

Like heifers in tiaras made by potters
who like to get things wrong and don't like tails,

adolescents in their underwear
would rather die than let themselves be handled.

Odonata

It starts before we're born and never stops
and very soon girls like me get lost

in air we try in vain to tiptoe backwards through
like dragonfly whose wings refuse to warm.

Ponies

We need to learn that all we need to do
is kiss our lovers like we kiss our ponies

which is hard
because they're not ponies.

Naturism

Think of it as wearing a bikini
made of nothing else but precious jewels;

think of it as thinking you're a vole
and waking up to find you're a windsock.

Torquay

Jazz is not appropriate for toddlers;
happiness is just a waste of time;

being friendly is naïve; murder
make the perfect subject for a book;

not to maintain resentment is morally supine
and women only *think* they like Torquay.

Facts and Figures

Facts and figures
work like a shrimping-net

shrimp, like salty greyhounds,
slip away from.

The Lives of Our Fathers

They live as if they can't and won't forgive
anybody anything ever,

least of all themselves for not inventing –
not even having dreamt of – umami.

Everything

They think it comes from them
but it doesn't,

it comes from Heaven
which explains everything.

Rats

I used to scream and scream
and when it rained

I ran outside
and screamed at the sky

but now I never scream
and my mouth

feels furry all the time like rats
searching blindly for the word for home.

What We Want

We've had to learn, and have to keep on learning,
there's more to life than doing what we want

and also – this is where it gets tricky –
to doing what the other person wants.

Dustmites

Housewives who say no to despair
are also saying no to the dustmites,

millions of them, living in their living-rooms –
and millions of dustmites can't be wrong.

Paranoia

Paranoia
tiptoes down our veins

like bees
that tiptoe down inside narcissi trumpets.

Iris

Hooded figures trundle wooden carts
up and down the valleys of their motherland

searching for the bones of their dear mothers
that glimmer in the mauvish light like iris bulbs,

bones they snatch and stow at top speed
as if the fact they're being dreamt enrages them.

Evening Out

Like people in their nineties shovelling snow
side by side on a dark night,

we're hoping that an evening out together
is saying what we want it to say!

What It Feels Like to Feel Like Me

It feels like my body has been trampled on
by herds of knitted cattle with felt ears –

which leaves me feeling curiously elated
for having been mistaken for a field.

Paradise

The women who they thought and think we ought to be
wait for them like salted trout or rabbit

waiting in their crates in the snow
for frozen men with frozen hearts in paradise.

BLOWFLY

Bridesmaids

Tiny bridesmaids trapped in borrowed boots
and stubbornly refusing to get up

sob into the mud like married men
sobbing on their beds in their suits.

Bath-time

Happy in the knowledge they are sweet
because they are too sweet to know how not to be,

they waltz about the bedrooms with no knickers on,
glistening with delicious–smelling unguents.

Meringues

They nibble their meringues like girls in shock,
white with sugar, mouthing the word 'nymph'.

Wives in Hats

Married men juggling large plates
push against the long narrow tables

where wives in hats are constantly reminding them
of everything they hate about themselves.

Teddybears

They used to sleep with teddybears but now
they sleep with men with skin and bone for fur.

Ducks

The married women in their dressing-gowns
who ask the rubber ducks with curly tails

why the mornings take so long to come
are asking the wrong ducks the wrong questions.

Tennis

Those who do their best no matter what
and only want a cuddle should play tennis.

Hubcaps

Married women's faces are like hubcaps
no one sees unless they're not there.

Nail-varnish

Upstairs in the bedrooms little bottles
huddle up together like young gnomes.

Salvation

Women marry men to be saved
though saved from what they have no idea.

Jam

They always feel sticky and their underwear
feels like it's made of spun jam.

Married Women Even at Their Gloomiest

Married women even at their gloomiest
never get too gloomy to be kind,

to offer cups of tea to every visitor,
however boring, often with a biscuit.

Breakfast Time

The married women rearranging bacon
on greasy plates as big as washing-up bowls

can hardly see the plates because the snow
comes right up to the top of the breakfast-room window-panes.

Profiteroles

Married women sometimes marry men
who like to treat their women like profiteroles.

God

God Who is in charge of fur and hair
sports a beard as fearsome as the wasps

that buzz about on men's infernal patios,
enraged by their refusal to be food.

Snails

The hearts of married women are like shells
shattered by the hooves of wild horses

thundering across deserted runways
where nothing moves except lethargic snails.

Bungalows

Married women love applying lip balm
to lips as dry as ornamental grasses

pointlessly rustling outside bungalows
that nobody has visited in years.

Representatives from the Milk Marketing Board

Married men
handle married women

like representatives from the Milk Marketing Board
whose only real interest is the blowfly.

Hopes

They toss their newfound hopes into the sky
then shoot them as they fall like newborn babies.

New Clothes

They buy themselves more and more new clothes
they know they'll never wear to meet the lovers

they know they'll never meet (they're not stupid)
who'll lean towards them from their sweating bays.

Horses with Gold Teeth

Like horses with gold teeth on greasy lunges
that circle in the sand of the riding-schools

of men in leather boots who work all night,
married women never get anywhere.

Tobogganist

Married life is fun – like eating gastropods
or trying to spell tobogganist is fun;

or being one, and ending up concussed
and on your way to another electroencephalogram.

Potatoes

They look like what potatoes would be like
if someone dressed potatoes in old dresses,

left them in a kitchen full of mouths
then turned the lights out for a hundred years.

How to Fish

Like starving people learning how to fish
they have to be so patient – and they are!

Years go by, they stay completely still –
but even then they never catch anything.

Desert Orchid

If Desert Orchid is a rhododendron,
and silkworms worms, a woman is a race-horse.

Tomorrow

They sit at home
dreaming of tomorrow

but when tomorrow comes
it's today.

Whiskers

They sometimes come across each other's husbands
wandering about like six-foot rabbits

who wonder what to do for entertainment
and how to wash and dry their twitchy whiskers.

Married Women on Holiday

They peer into their suitcases and wonder
if being dead is being still alive

but in a place miles away from anywhere
that nobody knows how to spell.

Travelodge

When you're dead you're dead and nothing matters
but when you're in a Travelodge it does.

Sunbathing

Lying on their backs in the sun,
they feel as if they'll never move again

like married women made entirely of egg yolk
feeling what it's like to feel hot.

The Nights of Married Women

The nights of married women
are like rooms

where nothing can survive
except succulents.

Sorrow

Sorrow also comes to those who pray –
it blocks their throats like golden boiled jewels.

Songbirds

It's not because they're sorry for the songbirds
but for themselves because they've got no soup.

Snowflake

This is what it's like to be a snowflake
or would be if it wasn't so hot.

To Pedal Round an Ornamental Lake

To pedal round an ornamental lake
among the ornamental ducks and lily-pads

when darkness closes in is to feel
all alone except for your knees.

The Less They Know

They don't know where or even what it is
or who to ask but the less they know

the more they are convinced that they belong there,
that they must try to get there, that they're missed.

High Dependency

Nobody wants to be alone here
and nobody wants to eat their soup

and nobody's got more than one neck
except for those who have now got two.

With Their Bony Fingers

With their bony fingers tiny mothers
are clinging to their sons as if they're pistols.

Married Women in Their Long Coats

Married women in their long coats
look like cards sent to the bereaved

by mourners the bereaved can't put a face to
who don't know what on earth they're meant to say.

Funeral

They walk like horses
walking through the mist

who know that God
created them to walk;

they walk beside the sides
of the ushers

who walk beside them
like devoted grooms.